Volume 3

BRITISH RAILWAYS IN COLOUR

Alan Earnshaw & Kevin Derrick

SOUTH

Nostalgia Road Publications

The **British Railways In Colour** Series ™

is produced under licence by

Nostalgia Road Publications Ltd.

Unit 6, Chancel Place

Shap Road Industrial Estate, Kendal LA9 6NZ

Tel. 01539 738832 - Fax: 01539 730075

designed and published by
Trans-Pennine Publishing Ltd.
PO Box 10,
Appleby-in-Westmorland,
Cumbria, CA16 6FA
Tel. 017683 51053 Fax. 017683 53558
e-mail: admin@transpenninepublishing.co.uk

and printed by
Kent Valley Colour Printers Ltd.
Kendal, Cumbria
01539 741344

© Trans-Pennine Publishing Ltd. 2004
Photographs: As credited

Front Cover: Seen here at Waterloo in 1964, 35029 *Ellerman Lines* basks in the warm sun as the crew chat together on the platform alongside. *Trans-Pennine Archive* (S88)

Rear Cover Top: Waiting to depart Southampton Central with an eclectic mixture of stock, 34056 Croydon is pictured waiting to leave with a special in 1963. *Trans-Pennine Archive* (S104)

Rear Cover Bottom: Considered ugly by many, the Bullied 0-6-0 Q1 class was a war-time creation that was devoid of running plates to lighten the load on the Southern's lightly-built branch line bridges ahead of the D-Day build-up. Twenty years later 33009 is seen taking on water at Waterloo, where it has arrived with a rake of empty stock. *Trans-Pennine Archive* (S202)

Title Page: At Milborne Port, 34099 West Country Class *Lynmouth* leads the 12.56 Salisbury - Yeovil working on 22nd August 1964. *Strathwood Library Collection* (S148)

This Page: Contrasting between one of the giants of steam, and a more humble member of the SR fleet we see 0-6-0T 30064 at Southampton. This was an American built locomotive from 1943, and brought to this country as support for the American forces ahead of D-Day. *Trans-Pennine Archive* (S152)

WELCOME to the third volume of the **British Railways in Colour** series, which deals with the Southern Region. The passing of steam from this region in 1967 was a major blow to steam enthusiasts and as the large Bullied engines were unceremoniously dragged off to scrapyards around the country, it seemed that only a few museum pieces would be left to tell the story of how imposing steam had been on the Southern!

Visitors to the National Railway Museum at York may find it hard to comprehend that the locomotive pictured on the front cover of this book, 35029 *Ellerman Lines*, is the one and the same engine that has been sectioned and put on display to demonstrate to visitors how a steam engine operated. At the time many questioned this, as they felt that very few reminders of the Southern Railway locomotive fleet would survive.

Above: *A wide-splasher variation of Drummond's T9 4-4-0, 30300 is seen at Eastleigh Works for repairs in 1960. It would be returned to Wadebridge shed for a final season, but most of the 'Greyhounds' would be gone by the end of 1961. Only 30120, with normal splashers would survive, as it too would eventually become part of the National Collection.*
Trans-Pennine Archive (S206)

Yet, thanks to Woodhams of Barry and the efforts of countless preservation schemes, Southern steam is arguably the backbone of Britain's preserved railways today. This book however presents a celebration of the region before it was drastically pruned of its locomotives in the mid-1960s. From Kent to Cornwall, this selection of colour images will transport the reader back to the days when steam reigned supreme.

Above: Underneath the footbridge at Whitchurch North we see a long-time Guildford engine U Class 2-6-0 31627, on 15th May 1964. Whitchurch had two stations, this one on the LSWR main line (which is still open) and one on the very useful north-south railway known as the Didcot, Newbury & Southampton (GWR line) which succumbed in 1960. *Strathwood Library Collection* (S110)

Right: Another view with a distinctive footbridge is that taken a day later at Dinton, as Merchant Navy Class 35003 *Royal Mail* passes through with an Exeter train. The neat and tidy station is representatitve of the period, with almost everything in its correct place. However, careful inspection will reveal that one of the fire buckets is missing! *Strathwood Library Collection* (S221)

Left: From 1962 onwards, the Bullied Pacific locomotives were starting to look very shabby, as the shortage of manpower at London steam depots (and elsewhere come to that) led to a cut-back in locomotive cleaning. The resulting shortage of cleaners meant that engines like 35021 *New Zealand Line* were turned out in a very poor external condition. Another contributing factor for the shabby state of the engine seen passing Brookwood (for Bisley Camp) with the 09.22 Bournemouth West to Waterloo, is the fact that it was just eight weeks away from withdrawal.
Strathwood Library Collection (S113)

Above: Calling at Templecombe with a stopping train Battle of Britain Class 4-6-2 34057 *Biggin Hill* is pictured in 1964. This was a well-travelled engine, and was new to Stewart's Lane in 1947, but it then went to Dover for a few months in 1948. In total it had 11 allocations, one of which was with the Eastern Region at Stratford, where it did a full year from May 1957 onwards to supplement the B1s. By the time of this view it was a Salisbury engine, and this was where it finished its working life in May 1967 before being sent to Cashmore's of Newport to be cut up that October.
Trans-Pennine Archive (S161)

Left: The rural station at Templecombe could hardly ever have been viewed as having much in common with our shot at Clapham Junction on this page. The M7 0-4-4T with a short smokebox was a Nine Elms (70A) engine for sometime, including 16th September 1961 when this picture was taken and a year before its withdrawal. The M7 was notionally allocated to Plymouth Friary (83H) in September 1962, but it seems unlikely that it went down to the Western Region as it was seen in Eastleigh Works in October 1962 and was scrapped there the following month. *Frank Hornby* (S89)

Above: As with the picture of the M7 at Clapham, the crew of U Class 2-6-0 31639 are seen in a moment of rest at Basingstoke in October 1965 before going back into Basingstoke Goods Yard. This has to be one of the most photographed Southern moguls, as it was one of the longest survivors and was constantly rostered on to specials as a consequence. Despite this it was not to escape into preservation and following withdrawal from Guildford (70C) it spent a short period in store at Eastleigh shed before being sent to Cashmore's of Newport for cutting in September 1966. *Strathwood Library Collection* (S116)

Top Left: The next batch of pictures could be titled 'Beside The Seaside' as we see two views taken at coastal resorts with engine sheds. The first was taken in September 1957 at Ramsgate, which was the shed 74B; but from October 1958 to June 1959 it was known as 73G, before it became an un-coded sub-shed of Ashford. It closed to steam in December 1960 and became an EMU stabling point. The locomotive seen here is a Maunsell N15 4-6-0, 30769 *Sir Balan*, which was a Stewarts Lane locomotive at the time of the view. It transferred to the Western Section in May 1959 and was allocated to Eastleigh (71A) but there can have been little work for it there, as it was withdrawn in February 1960 and cut up in the works shortly afterwards. *Alan Pike OBE* (S169)

Bottom Left: The next seaside shed to feature here is Bournemouth (70F), where this picture was taken in 1965. It shows a good line-up of Bullied locomotives, an Ivatt 2-6-2T, a Standard Class 5MT and what would be later classed as an 04 diesel shunter. The Merchant Navy Class 4-6-2 at the front of the group is 35007 *Aberdeen Commonwealth*, which was reputed to be one of the fastest locomotives of its class. As a consequence it was also a long-lived member of the class and lasted until the final week when it was withdrawn with a total of 1,318,765 miles under her belt (the highest in the class). After withdrawal from Nine Elms (70A) in July 1967, she was sent to Buttigieg's of Newport for cutting. *Strathwood Library Collection* (SH70)

Top Right: By contrast to the previous view, 34009 *Lyme Regis*, a re-built West Country Pacific did a total mileage of 959,762, with just 297,281 of those miles in its re-built form. It was therefore well short of *Aberdeen Commonwealth*'s final total when it was withdrawn on 2nd October 1966. Like 35007 it also went to the Newport yard of J. Buttigieg. In total 24 Bullied's met their end there, with six Merchant Navy's and 18 Battle of Britain/West Country locomotives sharing a similar destiny. The picture here shows *Lyme Regis* in happier days passing through Redbridge on 13.30 Waterloo to Weymouth train on 6th June 1965. Redbridge of course was also famous for the Southern Region sleeper works, and a thick smell of creosote always hung in the air as you passed by.
Strathwood Library Collection (S90)

Bottom Right: Providing a nice link between the two pictures on this page, we have two different examples of Southern signal boxes. Above, that at Redbridge has a hipped roof, whilst the one below has a gabled roof. This box was located at Farnborough North, and is pictured on 12th September 1964 as a Maunsell U Class 2-6-0, 31799, calls with the 13.50 Reading to Redhill express. Note the attractive nature of the station, with its various styles of architecture. Also of interest is the cream and green painted woodwork, the green and white enamelled sign for the gentleman's toilet and the concrete fence posts, all of which make an ideal form of inspiration to modellers.
Strathwood Library Collection (S150)

Above: The doyen of the Merchant Navy Class, 35001 *Channel Packet* is seen at Raynes Park on 27th June 1964 as it passes through with the Bournemouth Belle. Although this was still a prestigious working, it will be noted that the engine is far from clean, and this is again indicative of the shortage of cleaners at this time. This engine was one of the earlier casualties from the class and it was withdrawn just five months after this picture was taken. On withdrawal it was sent to Eastleigh and then on to Birds of Morriston for disposal. *Strathwood Library Collection* (S171)

Right: Another locomotive taking a through road at a station is Standard Class 5 4-6-0, 73161 running round at Yeovil Junction on 16th May 1964. The importance of this junction station is indicated by its size, and as can be seen a large covered footbridge spanned the tracks and platforms. One of your authors has an abiding memory of being stranded here for over 11 hours at Easter 1964, during which time train-spotting became a secondary interest to trying to keep warm! *Strathwood Library Collection* (S121)

Left: Another train seen taking a through road, is this up 'Holland America' special behind West Country Class 34103 *Calstock* passing through Brookwood on 4th June 1965. Again we see a somewhat untidy engine, which by this time is just three months from its withdrawal from Eastleigh in September 1965. After a period of time in store at Eastleigh it was sent north to Buttigiegs of Newport for cutting in April 1966. Note the BIL set on an up stopping train to the right of the West Country loco as it speeds past.
Strathwood Library Collection (S122)

Above: In contrast to the previous picture, we see the roles of steam and modern traction reversed at Fleet in Hampshire on the same day. This time it is a steam working that calls into the platform road, behind BR Standard Class 5 4-6-0 73018 on the 13.12 Basingstoke to Waterloo semi-fast. The through road is being used by Warship class diesel D866 *Zebra* on the 10.30 Exeter - Waterloo express, at a time when these Swindon-built Class 42s were taking over from the Merchant Navies that were being withdrawn.
Strathwood Library Collection (B259)

Above: The swan-song years of the Merchant Navy Class provides our next picture at Axminster on 17th May 1964. Featured here is 35024 *East Asiatic Company,* which would last barely seven months after this view was taken. The engine would be ultimately cut up by Woodfield's of Town Dock Newport. Furthermore this was just a part of the changing face of the railways and very soon station scenes like this would also be gone, as many country stations were closed or reduced to the status of un-staffed halts.
Strathwood Library Collection (S200)

Right: Still at Axminster, this time with even more antiquated stock, we see the branch train for Lyme Regis behind an Adams 0-4-4T tank, 30583 in June 1959. Passengers' luggage will have been transferred to the branch train, as it prepares to trundle down the 6¾miles to the south coast. The branch was a casualty of Beeching and it closed in November 1965, despite dieselisation with Western Region multiple units. The Adams tanks gave way to Ivatt 2-6-2Ts in 1960, but 30583 went on into preservation.
the late Norman Browne, Strathwood Library Collection (S123)

Above: Another route that saw the arrival of several members of the ex-LMS Ivatt 2-6-2 tank engine class was the Brighton to Horsham services. Here we see 41223 in exile with the 11.30 from Brighton on 28th July 1963. There is quite a lot to say about the transfer of these engines following the progressive introductions of DMUs on their former territory, but for the moment we would like to say something about the glorious line up of vehicles seen outside Southwick Station. Parked on the forecourt, from left to right we have a Morris J-Type van, and Austin 8 saloon, a Morris Minor Series MM, a Rover P3 and an Austin-Morris Mechanical Horse. A period Royal Mail letterbox and Lambretta scooter complete the scene. Parked on the road, is 1255 BP, a Ford Consul Hi-line De-luxe model first registered in West Sussex in April 1958. It is finished in the Ford colours of Ivory and Hereford Green, and carries the optional extras of a sun visor and spot lamps. For more on vehicles of this kind, we invite you to read the Nostalgia Road book, *Ford Motor Cars 1945-1964*. *Strathwood Library Collection* (M2)

Below: Another view of the competition between railway travel and private motoring is seen at Burseldon near Southampton. Crossing the road is 34032 *Camelford* working the 09.30 Waterloo - Bournemouth service. Prominent in the foreground are a pair of Rootes Group cars, with a Hillman Super Minx estate on the left and a Singer Gazelle on the right, whilst a 15-cwt Commer van (also by Rootes) can be seen on the far side of the bridge. A Nostlagia Road book on Rootes products is due to appear soon!
Strathwood Library Collection (S100)

Top Left: Cutting contrasts are seen in this pair of pictures, first of all at Mortehoe on the Ilfracombe branch as 34054 *Lord Beaverbrook* on the 16.30 Ilfracombe to Exeter Central on 2nd August 1964. Whereas the generation who saw the introduction of the Battle of Britain Class would need no introduction to the person who this locomotive was named after, today's generation might think it out of place from the names of famous airfields, RAF squadrons or famous aircraft like the Hurricane or Spitfire. Perhaps some will associate the name Beaverbrook with a Pier of the Realm who was a wealthy newspaper magnate. Whilst that is true, Beaverbrook's claim to fame on the side of a locomotive was solely due to his role of Minister of Aircraft Production during the dark days of war. It was his undoubted strength in organising the manufacture and supply of both fighter and bomber aircraft in the troubled times of the early 1940s that helped this country win the Battle of Britain.
Strathwood Library Collection (S125)

Bottom Left: Another Battle of Britain Class engine, 34057, *Biggin Hill*, is seen at Buckhorn Weston. These views show interesting aspects of trackside maintenance at this location, with the upper view demonstrating quite clearly the burning of overgrowth. The second view shows how drainage channels have been cut down the slopes of the cutting, and then filled with rocks and ballast as a means of preventing landslides.
Strathwood Library Collection (S151)

Above: From country to town, the Merchant Navy class were to be found in diverse settings, and the contrast between Buckhorn Weston and Nine Elms is quite appreciable from this 1962 picture of 35003 Royal Mail. The flats in the background offered quite a vantage over the railway yard, but equally they were the source of some complaints about loco crews; so a large notice at the end of the yard read 'make no smoke or noise'. It may seem strange to relate, that when the original line into London was opened, that it was Nine Elms that was the terminus and not Waterloo!

Trans-Pennine Archive (S99)

Above: Romsey in Hampshire is the setting for this view of a Standard Class 5 73093 on 8th May 1965 as it heads the 11.47 Salisbury - Chichester goods working. The station opened in March 1847, and whilst it still has passenger facilities, the goods facilities there closed in July 1970. *Strathwood Library Collection* (B339)

Right: On the same day we see Dunbridge station, but this was an early casualty as far as freight was concerned, losing its facilities in 1961. This is therefore a through freight (from Salisbury to Eastleigh), the Standard Class 5 73082 at its head is now preserved on the Bluebell Railway as *Camelot*. *Strathwood Library Collection* (B302)

Above: The BR Standard Class 5s took over a lot of the work on the Southern Region that had formerly been done by the King Arthur and Lord Nelson classes, although some of these continued well into the early 1960s. One of the 1962 Lord Nelson survivors, 30864 *Sir Martin Frobisher,* is seen here at Clapham Junction in August 1959 with a down train. *Strathwood Library Collection* (S131)

Right: Just a short walk across to the Windsor side at Clapham Junction could lead the visitor to a scene of careful shunting as glass-lined milk tanks were prepared for their journey back to the country creameries. Here we see one of the rarer M7 0-4-4Ts, 30123, with its longer frames and short smokebox in September 1958. *the late Norman Browne, Strathwood Library Collection* (S105)

Above: By catching a Windsor line train and travelling to Feltham, a long walk would then take you to Feltham Shed (70B). However, it seems that few photographers ever bothered taking colour images at this location (although we'd be happy for you to prove us wrong)! The shed was quite an interesting place to visit, especially after the Kent Coast Electrification, as some of the withdrawn locomotives were stored there. One such engine was D1 class 4-4-0, 31246, which is captured by the camera on 25th October 1959 along with fellow D1 31545. It will be seen that the chimneys have been covered with canvas as part of the storage process, perhaps in anticipation of the prospect of being returned to work. Indeed a few of them did enjoy a brief respite at the end of that year on Christmas parcels traffic but for 4-4-0s as a whole, the time left was very limited indeed. Note the aircraft passing to the left of the chimney, indicating the close proximity of the shed and Heathrow Airport. *Strathwood Library Collection* (S108)

Below: Staying at Feltham, we see another class that was also stored at this location. This time we visit the shed in February 1962 to witness a line up of three locomotives that were already consigned to history. From left to right we have a 700 class 0-6-0 30346, a G16 4-8-0T 30494 and a W Class 2-6-4T 31923. All three of these engines would meet their end (after being consigned to Eastleigh Works) between March 1963 and August 1963.

A feature of the G16 tank are its cut-down side tanks that were fitted to allow better visibility for the shunting work they had to undertake. They were designed especially for work at Feltham Marshalling Yards, but were originally delivered to the Strawberry Hill Depot in 1921 and transferred to Feltham when the yard opened there in 1922, a year ahead of its coming into full operation.
Trans-Pennine Archive (S120)

Above: Obviously inspiration from the G16 was carried into Maunsell's Z Class 0-8-0T, which was introduced from March 1929 onwards. Eight of these powerful tank engines were built at the Southern's Brighton Works. Envisaged as banking engines, they were not as successful at the duty as had been envisaged and they therefore became powerful shunters. On Nationalisation 30951 was allocated with four other members of the class to Hither Green, but it was at Ashford (73F) when it ended its days in November 1962. It is seen here at Eastleigh Works during an overhaul in 1959, but would return to the works for cutting five years later. *Trans-Pennine Archive* (S137)

Above: Richard Maunsell went on to produce a 2-6-4T from his N Class 2-6-0 Mogul in the early 1930s. Named the W Class, these engines acquired a four-wheeled trailing bogie, which unusually had integral braking designed from the outset. At nationalisation the engine was allocated to Stewarts Lane, where we see it pictured in 1962.

It had a number of allocations in the years that followed, but at the time of this view it was based at Norwood Junction (75C). It ended its days at Exmouth Junction (83D) as a banker at Exeter Central, and was withdrawn from there in October 1963 before being cut up a month later at Eastleigh. *Trans-Pennine Archive* (S136)

Left: In a similar location to one of the pictures on the rear cover, we see re-built West Country, 34012 *Launceston* at Southampton Central in 1963. Both the station canopy and the locomotive are looking decidedly untidy, and no doubt the interior of the coaches would not be too clean either. It was as if the railway was in its death throes, as conditions like these certainly deterred many passengers of the day from travelling by rail.
Trans-Pennine Archive (S106)

Above: Another really grubby locomotive, this time an un-rebuilt West Country loco, 34023 *Blackmore Vale*, on the 10.30 Poole - York train on 4th June 1966. It is seen passing Winchester and the small engine shed at that location can just be seen to the rear of the train. The engine would end its BR service on 9th July 1967, and was therefore destined for private preservation. It went first to storage at the Longmoor Military Railway and then down to the Bluebell Railway. *Strathwood Library Collection* (S159)

Top Left: One of the biggest changes that would befall the railway, but is remarkably noticeable in many of our photographs, would be the levels of rail-born traffic that were handled by even very small local stations. This type of traffic is clearly seen at Cosham on 19th June 1965, as the 11.06 Portsmouth and Southsea to Fareham stopping service calls behind BR Standard Class 4MT, 76066, which is fitted with the BR1B tender. Before long however, the parcels traffic would be decimated, especially when BR abandoned its road delivery service in 1968. Thereafter the platforms would be largely bare of this staple form of traffic.
Strathwood Library Collection (B260)

Bottom Left : By way of contrast, the platforms at Hook in Hampshire are totally bare of any parcels traffic when our photographer visited the station on 4th June 1965. A re-built Merchant Navy Pacific, 35023 *Holland-Afrika Line*, is working the 14.45 Waterloo to Exeter relief
Strathwood Library Collection (S112)

Right: A cleaner Merchant Navy, 35010 *Blue Star*, appears on a goods train at Yeovil Junction on 16th May 1964. A picture of this class of locomotive on this kind of duty is quite unusual, despite the fact that they were officially classed as a mixed traffic engine; this being the reason given for the sanction for their building during World War II. Yet, despite this, colour photographs of Merchant Navy engines on freights are few and far between.
Strathwood Library Collection (S153)

Above: On page 3 we saw one of the variety of T9s with the wide splashers, but here we have one of the earlier Drummond 4-4-0 'Greyhounds' coming into Fareham with a rake of SR green stock on 24th August 1957. The engine is 30718, which lasted in steam at Exmouth Junction until March 1961, whereupon it was moved to Eastleigh Works to be cut up a month later. The T9s were replaced by BR Standards (mostly 4MT 2-6-4Ts and 2-6-0 Moguls), and by the summer of 1963 T9 30120 was the last British standard gauge 4-4-0 still on the BR stock list.
Strathwood Library Collection (S92)

Right: One of the replacement BR Standards working a duty formerly undertaken by the T9s is seen here with Standard Class 4 2-6-0 76059 on 12th June 1965 at Fareham on what was the last day of steam at this location. It was on the 10.35 Cardiff - Portsmouth with a long rake of maroon BR MkI carriages behind. The replacement stock for this line would be the Eastleigh-built 2-car or 3-car diesel multiple units for the locals, although the longer distance trains like that to Cardiff would fall to Hymeks or the Swindon-built cross-country DMU sets.
Strathwood Library Collection (B303)

Left: Wilton Station is the brief host to a Salisbury stopper with a BR Standard Class 4MT 2-6-0, 76007, at its head on 16th May 1964. Originally two stations served this town famous for the carpet trade, but the former GWR station of Wilton North closed in 1955, allowing Wilton South seen here to become plain Wilton. Careful examination of building styles reveal an unusual mix of both brick and dressed stone, together with the use of slates on the walls to protect against damp and pre-cast concrete platform edges. *Strathwood Library Collection* (B261)

Above: Although 76007 was a Salisbury (70E) engine, it has found its way to the ash roads at Fratton on 10th July 1966. At one time this shed on the outskirts of Portsmouth had been coded 71D having been built jointly by the London & South Western Railway and the London, Brighton & South Coast Railway. By the 1950s the effects of the electric units on the 'Pompey' line had seen it recoded in 1954 to 70F before it officially closed to steam on 2nd November, 1959. However, as can be seen, steam could always be found here right up to the end! *J.R. Beddows* (B300)

Above: As well as ash facilities, the provision of water for engines was made not only at engine sheds but at many stations as well; especially where the diagram would allow for crew changes or the passage of faster traffic. This shot at Barnstaple from 1960 provides a good example as West Country Pacific, 34011 *Tavistock*, has a clear road signalled ahead, so the fireman can now return the water crane's bag to its normal position and jump down again. *Tavistock* was one of those not to be rebuilt and was unfortunate to be in the first wave of withdrawals from her class on 30th November, 1963 as an Exmouth Junction (72A) engine and sent to Eastleigh Works for disposal by April 1964. *Trans Pennine Archive* (S124)

Right: Whilst it was a warm sunny day in the previous picture, it must be pretty cold at Feltham (70B); note that there is frost on the ground and a mix of fine ash from the fire devil and frost around the water column at this former London & South Western Railway shed. By February 1965, many of the older pre-Grouping railways locomotives had already been withdrawn and their places taken by both diesels and BR Standards. This 4MT 2-6-4T, 80069, was based at nearby Nine Elms (70A), and if the headcode is to be believed, she would have worked light engine to Feltham after working in one of the area's station goods yards. Her sister locomotive behind, 80148, was on her home shed at the time. *Strathwood Library Collection* (B304)

Top Left: Continuing our look at BR Standards on the Southern Region, we now see another engine based at Nine Elms (70A), as 80154 performs empty stock duties in the busy carriage yards at Clapham Junction. These sidings, located in the 'V' of the tracks between the main station and the Windsor lines was (and still is) a place of much activity throughout the day. Several engines would be seen here on any visit during the 1950s and '60s. For many years these turns would have been performed by M7 0-4-4Ts, before these were ousted in the early sixties by a small allocation of ex GWR 57xx 0-6-0PTs sent to Nine Elms. These were as outsiders not popular with all the crews, their hungry appetite for coal and water made them a poor replacement for the LSWR engines and they were ultimately replaced by Standards. *Trans Pennine Archive* (B262)

Bottom Left: A much scruffier Nine Elms engine, a BR Standard Class 3MT 2-6-2T, 82029, is found sharing the same duties in 1965. There was a bigger allocation of these 3MT tanks here at this time, and as some of these had migrated in from the Western Region some retained their green livery. Engine cleaners were a very rare breed indeed at 70A and many of these locomotives began to appear in a shocking condition with limescale stains appearing down their tanks. Many of these locomotives stayed on these duties up to July 1967 when the Bournemouth line was electrified. *Trans Pennine Archive* (B301)

Top Right: Merchant Navy Pacific, 35027 *Port Line* clearly reinforces the need for cleaners as she coasts through Clapham Junction towards Waterloo with one of the premier trains in the whole country 'The Bournemouth Belle'. The lack of cleaners must also have been the case at Bournemouth MPD (70F) as this was Port Line's home shed. Hopefully there were enough cleaners available for the carriage sidings at both Clapham Junction and Branksome in Bournemouth where the Pullman cars were serviced. The lead vehicle is one of the 57 foot full brakes specially repainted to at least try and preserve the image of this prestigous train which, along with steam, vanished from the Southern in July 1967.
Strathwood Library Collection (S107)

Bottom Right: Given the state of steam locomotives at that time, the esteemed shedmaster Dick Hardy at Stewarts Lane (73A) was perhaps fortunate that the other great named train on the region, the 'Golden Arrow' had gone over to electric working in 1961. Towards the end of steam working on the Kent routes, we gain an impression of what a prestige train should look like. Here we see one of the regulars on the Golden Arrow, West Country Class 34101 Hartland, on 31st March 1961. This was actually a Bricklayers Arms (73B) engine at this time, and looks in fine fettle as it strides out of Victoria Station and begins it ascent up the short but rather steep (1:62) Grosvenor Bank.
Frank Hornby (S162)

Left: At the other end of the scale for Southern Region engines, we see one of William Stroudleys A1X 0-6-0Ts, 32662 standing in the rain outside the coachworks at Lancing on 5th May 1962. At that date this example was allocated to Brighton (75A), and was a member of a class that was popular with both enthusiasts and crews alike. However, Lancing Works would have been missed by many spotters of the day, even though a visit there was truly fascinating. Once named *Martello*, this 1875-built little engine thankfully made it into preservation.
Strathwood Library Collection (S114)

Above: Famed for the weight restrictions on the Langstone Bridge, the branch to Hayling Island left Havant near the former London Brighton & South Coast Railway station. Originally Havant was served by another station on the London & South Western Railway until the stations were merged in 1859. An A1X 0-6-0T from Eastleigh (71A), 32661, is taking the branch on a sunny 6th August 1961. Despite the delays to road traffic at the crossing gates and the enormous cost of maintaining the famous swing bridge, the Hayling Island branch would have made a wonderful preserved line. *Strathwood Library Collection* (S155)

Above: Further along the mainline we reach Portsmouth & Southsea, a spot much ignored by enthusiasts but very busy none the less, especially due to the naval dockyards. It was probably the fact that the main line from Waterloo was electrified back in 1937 (with the use of units like the 4-COR and 4-BUF sets) that many steam enthusiasts ignored the town. Furthermore the early closure of the town's steam shed at Fratton (70F) makes it unusual to see much colour material at this location. So the appearance of Battle of Britain Pacific 34088 *213 Squadron*, even one bereft of name and number plates, is worthy of our attention. Ironically the unit on the left is a diesel multiple unit that would find its way back along non-electrified lines to Wichester via Botley.
Alan Pike OBE (S126)

Right: The eastern section into Kent was electrified in 1961, so there is also a shortage of colour material from this area. Even so, we visit Ashford in May 1959, where we see 31876, one of the Maunsell three-cylinder N1 Class moguls. Although she does not carry a shed plate yet the engine has just been transferred this month from Hither Green (73C) to Tonbridge (73J). The electrification of the Kent lines, together with the wanton keeness to go forward with the Beeching plan, led to a wholesale slaughter of the region's steam stock. In October and November 1962 the six remaining N1s were placed into store pending scrapping; 31876 eventually found its way to Eastleigh Works for cutting in October of 1963.
Trans Pennine Archive (S101)

Top Left: Another of Richard Maunsell's three-cylinder Moguls were the U1 class, which the Southern began building at Easteligh in 1931. However, once they left the works they were never really associated with Eastleigh or the Western section again, at least for about 30 years, and the end of their working lives. Until then most of their works' visits were to Ashford on the Eastern section, as seen with 31895 on 25th February 1962. This engine was still on the books of Redhill (75C) when it went in to the works, although it transferred to Stewarts Lane (75D) on release. Just ten months later it joined most of its classmates, being stored in the open at Hove Goods Yard for seven months, before being sent back to Eastleigh for cutting in August 1963. *Strathwood Library Collection* (S203)

Bottom Left: Sister engine, 31896 was also based at Redhill (75C) at the time of this July 1961 picture, although it is seen at Stewarts Lane then coded 73A. On 17th June 1962, this shed became 75D in one of the many changes of that period. With less power than the smaller wheeled N and N1 class locos, many of the class migrated first of all to Western section sheds after their displacement from Kent in May 1961, this one going first to Feltham (70B). Within a few months they all found their way to Central section sheds, but 17 of the 21-strong class were taken out of service in the 1962 cull. In addition to Eastleigh, three members of the class (31893, 31894 and 31996) were cut up by the private scrapyard of A. King & Son, Norwich. *Trans Pennine Archive* (S156)

Above: The Southern Railway had its own distinctive station furniture and target signs of the kind witnessed here at Woking, indeed many of the region's stations were never to receive BR totems after nationalisation. Even after station signs were removed from the Southern during the dark days of World War II, their post war replacements were to the original pattern. Another product from the Eastleigh works during this time, were the Merchant Navy Class Pacifics. Emerging as 21C3 on 13th September 1941, this engine was named *Royal Mail* in a ceremony at Waterloo by Lord Essendon, the Chairman of The Royal Mail Lines on 24th October 1941. The first shed for the new engine was to be Salisbury, but she got around seven further allocations in her service life including a stint as a Western Region engine in 1963 when Exmouth Junction (72A) transferred from the Southern Region and became 83D. Nationalisation saw the change of number to 35003, and 11 years later she was rebuilt! Lasting to the end of Southern Region steam in July 1967, she was put in storage at Nine Elms until a final journey saw her being moved to J. Cashmore Ltd of Newport, South Wales in December of 1967.
Strathwood Library Collection (S102)

Top Left: Yet another Bullied Pacific to end its days in a South Wales scrapyard was West Country Class 34020 *Seaton.* This Bullied Pacific was only to have two sheds in its entire working life, and as such was unique. It was first allocated to Exmouth Junction when new in 1945 before spending 11 years at Nine Elms from April 1951 onwards. Finally it went back to Exmouth Junction again in May 1962 and a month later, she is seen at Barnstaple Junction.
Trans Pennine Archive (S117)

Bottom Left: Also at Barnstaple Junction in June 1962, and with the fireman just about to pick up the token, is West Country Class 34038 *Lynton.* A busy location at times with, as its name suggests, several lines coming together here, most notably the mainline back along the withered arm to Exeter and the Barnstaple – Ilfracombe branch. Another line to diverge at Barnstaple, was that which ran east and south to Bideford and Torrington. These North Devon lines were the preserve of the un-rebuilt light Pacifics, and they made an incongruous sight in the winter months when they could often be observed with just a few coaches in tow. From Barnstaple a former GWR line ran east to Taunton, and it is on this latter route that the Churchward Mogul, 6372, would work and as such it is fitted with a tablet catcher. The name of the West Country locomotive, Lynton, is of course appropriate as the narrow gauge line to Lynton ran north-east from Barnstaple.
Trans Pennine Archive (S170)

Top Right: Nine Elms is our next location, with an undated picture from 1962. There we find one of R.J. Billington's E4 Class 0-6-2Ts, 32473, which dates from late-Victorian times in a design from 1898. Originally numbered B473 (later becoming 2473), she was to continue a long service life after moving here from Bricklayers Arms (73B), where she had previously been a long term resident. With a power classification of 2P/2F her classmates would have spent their early years on suburban passenger duties around London. As the electrification of these routes advanced many of the survivors found further work on local goods and shunting duties. This example was to find a role again on passenger workings on the Bluebell Railway, where she was ultimately preserved after her withdrawal in November 1962.
Trans Pennine Archive (S93)

Bottom Right: Another product from a Victorian railway, the South Eastern & Chatham, was Harry Wainwright's C Class 0-6-0. An example of this 2F power classification, 31578, is seen on 27th February 1960 at Stewarts Lane (73A). With a tender piled high with coal, she is playing about in the shed yard. Originally there were no less than 109 of these simple efficient freight locomotives that were built from 1900 onwards. As can be seen from the background, a small fleet of electric locomotives were serviced here, but there was a need to keep such 'high-tec' locomotives out of the grimy steam shed environment.
Strathwood Library Collection (S132)

Left: The other main constituent of the Southern Railway was the London & South Western Railway, one of whose designers was the frighteningly strict Dugald Drummond. His first new locomotive in 1897 was the M7 0-4-4T, one of which, 30055, is found near Rowfant in 1961. In February 1964 this locomotive emulated her designer, as both were destined to end their days at Eastleigh. Just over 51 years earlier, on 7th December 1912, the 72-year old Drummond was badly scalded at the works and he passed away the next day. He was later buried at Brookwood Cemetery within just a few yards of the mainline.
Strathwood Library Collection (S111)

Above: Gravesend Central Station is found on the North Kent line, and close by a ferry connects the town to Tilbury Riverside Station in Essex on the northern bank of the River Thames. At Gravesend Central two of Harry Wainwrights H Class 0-4-4Ts are seen, as they are engaged in changing over locomotives for working the branch to the once sparsley populated Allhallows-on-Sea. The branch was served on this day in 1960, by two of Tonbridge's (73J) roster of H's 31517 and 31553, however this was not a scene that would last much longer as the branch lost regular passenger and goods facilities on 4th December 1961.
The Late Norman Browne, Strathwood Library Collection (S142)

Top Left: Another pair of the H Class engines are seen on shed at Tonbridge (73J) on 17th April 1960. In the background we see 31266 from Tunbridge Wells West (73F), whilst 31305 was a Bricklayers Arms (73B) engine at the time. The characteristic Pagoda' roof-style of cab is apparent in these shots on these lightly powered 1P locomotives. Originally supplied for suburban passenger work from 1904, thus allowing the driver to keep dry on rainy days when looking out for the guards right o' way at the stations they called at. Note how high the coal is piled in the bunker of 31305, and it is likely that quite a lot of this would fly off as the engine went along.
Strathwood Library Collection (S157)

Bottom Left: Fortunately one of the H Class was to survive and again thanks to the efforts of those early preservationists and that engine, 31263 proudly wears her Ashford (74A) shed plate when seen on the same day at a very busy Tonbridge MPD. Prior to 13th October 1958, Tonbridge (73J) was coded as 74D, but it was to close completely in January 1965. Electrification and closures having taken their toll, the last few steam engines based there passed to Tunbridge Wells West until the following June when the Central division officially ousted itself of steam. Today steam in Kent is just a memory, but the Kent & East Sussex Railway keeps alive those memories a few miles south-east of Tonbridge.
Strathwood Library Collection (SH103)

Top Right: Two museum pieces are seen at Hampton Court (which is deep in electric territory) on 16th December 1962. Three of these 0298 Class 2-4-0Ts made it into British Railways' ownership. They were 30585, 30586 and 30587, and all were based at Wadebridge in Cornwall on nationalisation. Aside from the station shunts at Wadebridge these engines have also been much photographed on the Wenford Bridge china clay trains. They were originally part of a much larger class designed by Beattie for the London & South Western Railway in 1874 but based on an even earlier design; over the years that followed they were rebuilt by Adams, Urie and Maunsell. To mark the passing of the class, the remaining pair ran two special workings around the London suburban area.
Strathwood Library Collection (S154)

Bottom Right: The branch to Padstow, like Wadebridge, was to close on 30th January 1967 despite the fact that it was one of the earliest railways to open in the West Country on 4th July 1834. Such longevity was not to be for Maunsells N class Mogul 31845 seen at the Cornish terminus in 1962, although a commendable 40 years was achieved. With two coaches for Halwill Junction in the County of Devon; as this was almost 50 miles and 11 intermediate stations away, the passengers would be in for a long ride. The Mogul's last journey would be to Birds of Morriston, where she was sent from Exmouth Junction (83D) at the end of 1964.
Trans Pennine Archive (S127)

Left: Two stars of many of the railtours towards the end of Southern Region steam, were U class Moguls 31791 and 31639. The former was rebuilt from a River Class 2-6-4T, following the Sevenoaks accident of 1927. By the time they are pictured passing a Standard 5MT 4-6-0 at Woking 30th April 1966, the pair only had a few more weeks to go. The Reading to Redhill line was their last stomping ground, along with the last few N Moguls based out of Guildford (70C). By September of 1966 this pair had sadly found their way to Cashmores of Newport for cutting up.
The Late Norman Browne, Strathwood Library Collection (S165)

Above: There is no mistaking that we are still at Woking, as this sign was provided by the railway for its passengers. Illuminated at night, the upkeep of the bulbs would have been a duty for the Signal & Telegraph Department. The Standard 5MT 4-6-0, 73118, was a 1955 Doncaster-built engine that inherited the name *King Leodegrance* from the 1957 withdrawn Urie King Arthur class 4-6-0 30739. However by May 1967, this was academic as all the plates had disappeared from the locomotive, and even some of the tender rivets were letting water by judging from the stains.
Strathwood Library Collection (B338)

Top Left: Improvements to the designs of locomotives sometimes contributed to the comfort of engine crews and sometimes the reverse. When originally built, many of the N class moguls did not have the benefit of smoke deflectors. Richard Maunsell's careful design to not impede the driver's vision is well illustrated at St.Kew Highway on 1st August 1961. Running in the opposite direction with a Padstow train is West Country Pacific 34015 *Exmouth*.
Strathwood Library Collection (S143)

Bottom Left: An unidentified Bullied rebuild is having ash raked out from the smoke box at Nine Elms just along from one of the Q1 0-6-0s 33009. Modifications to these engines were few, except the fitting of AWS. This would be useful on these as with their lightweight tenders they had far more trouble stopping heavy freights on falling gradients.
Bob Treacher Alton Model Centre (S172)

Right: Standing leisurely at lonely Petrockstow, with its lovely barley twist lamp and wild rhododendrons, Ivatt 2MT 2-6-2T 41216 is working the 20-mile Halwill Junction to Torrington line on 12th June 1964. Look at the vision the crew would enjoy when working bunker-first, then compare this with other tank engine designs in the companion volume on the London Midland Region. These were great little engines from a crew's position, and they spawned both the Standard 2MT and 3MT 2-6-2Ts .
Strathwood Library Collection (M76)

Above: Modified by Maunsell from the original design of the S15 Class 4-6-0 by Urie, is 30824 seen here at Feltham (70B) in September 1965. Several designs of tender were tried on the S15s, the earliest of these was a 1920-pattern inside-framed eight-wheeled 'water cart' type; most of which had been scrapped by the mid-1950s. Urie designed a 5,200-gallon double bogie pattern and this was more or less copied by Maunsell with a 5,000-gallon version that became popular with Western section crews. Those locomotives within the class that had come over from the Eastern section at Ashford with six-wheeled 4,000-gallon tenders, were not well liked even though they rode better.

After the war most of the six-wheeled tenders were changed for redundant double-bogie tenders from the withdrawn King Arthurs. Even though Richard Maunsell was from the Eastern Section, and was responsible for sorting out the apparent mess left by his predecessor Harry Wainwright, it was the works at Eastleigh and not Ashford that were chosen to build his batch of 25 locomotives. Built in three batches from 1927 onwards, 30824 would be in the first batch. Following the Depression, the last was to enter traffic in December 1936, but only after financial assistance from the government.

Win Wall, Strathwood Library Collection (S133)

Above: A design that was generally well thought of by most Southern enginemen were the Maunsell N Class Moguls. Many regarded locomotives such as 31810 as being 'just right', but it has also obviously gained the admiration of a couple of lads standing on the platform at Ashford in Kent. This 1959 working would have been a London Bridge to Dover stopping train, and it is ready to depart on the final leg of its journey. The rapid acceleration demonstrated by the N Class, especially with four coach loads is fondly remembered. Following the successful electrification of the Portsmouth line in 1937, services such as this would surely have gone over from steam much earlier.

However, World War II intervened, and passenger services through Kent underwent a massive sea change, especially following the cessation of the English Channel steamer services in early 1940. Following the fall of Dunkirk, and the implementation of Operation Dynamo, the N Class locos were in the thick of moving evacuated troops to safety. The locomotive's designer, Richard Maunsell retained his association with Ashford after his retirement as the Southern Railway's Chief Mechanical Engineer in 1937, he remained in the area up until his death in 1944 and was later buried in the town's Bybrook Cemetery.
Trans Pennine Archive (S172)

Above: *To close this volume we see a rake of six-wheeled milk tankers behind West Country Class, 34009* Lyme Regis *passing through Grateley at quite a rate of knots on Friday 15th May 1964. In contrast to many of her sisters, the Pacific looks reasonably turned out for this day's duties.*
Strathwood Library Collection (S118)

EVERY PICTURE is worth a thousand words, or so they say, and thanks to the combined talents of photographers who have supplied material to both the Strathwood and Trans-Pennine archives, we have a lot to say in future volumes. Of course it would not have been possible to tell this story without the kind co-operation of the contributors named in the credits shown in this book.

To those and all those who captured British Railways In Colour, we say a massive thank you! However mere words are never enough, and we hope that the ongoing series will provide a testimony to the far-sighted work.

In conclusion, can we offer a reminder that all of these published shots are available to purchase as superb duplicate slide copies direct from Strathwood. The code number at the end of each slide indicates its catalogue number, and also the name of the photographer whose work we felt warranted inclusion.

To get your copy of the extensive catalogue listing of these and many thousands of other shots available in fabulous colour, please send £5.00 to: -

> Strathwood Limited
> Kirkland House
> Bruce Street, Whithorn.
> Dumfries & Galloway DG8 8PY

Or visit the websites: -
www.strathwood.com or www.railwayslide.co.uk.
In return we will send the collector's catalogue, complete with sample slide, post free to UK address (overseas add £2.50).